With Lavender Tea

E.E. Sorrells

With Lavender Tea

Copyright © 2023 Eryn Elizabeth Sorrells

All rights reserved. No part of the publication may be reproduced without written permission from the author.

ISBN: 978-1-7363658-6-1 (Paperback)

Library of Congress Control Number: 2023922195

Published in La Vergne, TN 37086 USA

Written by E.E. Sorrells

Cover image by Amira S.

First Published 2024

To my support system.

To my readers.

And

To myself,

As selfish as that might be.

Trigger Warning:

This book contains—but is not limited to—themes of

suicide,

self-harm,

suicidal thoughts,

rape,

sexual assault,

abuse,

harassment,

depression,

anxiety,

hallucinations,

eating disorders,

etc.

Please use caution in proceeding and remember to practice self-love at all times. If any urges to hurt yourself or others arise, seek help from local or national hotlines.

Enjoy the read!

Table of Contents

Dusk..i
- What's Mine..1
- The Worth of Gold...1
- Strung Up..1
- Dear Flowers: Part Two...2
- Leaving My Home Church..3
- Mushrooms...4
- Signed by a Lost Lover...5
- Becoming a Star..6
- The Last Goodbye...7
- Colors..8
- Am I Really Enough?..8
- The Blessed Tomorrow...8
- Cry More...9
- Numbers..10
- Loving Sleep...13
- Maybe in the Future..13
- You Don't Deserve to See Me Now............................13
- I've Never Liked Puzzles..14
- Is there such a thing?..15
- Lemon Wedges...15
- Advice to a Younger "E"..16
- Walking Horse Words..17
- From Nature to Now...18
- Is our Civilization, Civilized?....................................19
- What I've done to Myself...20
- Wreckage..21

Dream Boy	21
My Sizzled Out Candle	22
An Ode to My Life	23
The Mysterious Fossils of the Past	25
Thinning	26
Life is a School	27
Tired Again	28
Distraction 1	29
Sleeping Without Me	29
Cocktails	30
Too Many Questions	31
Preparation	31
Gifts	32
Wishes for You	32
Abandonment	33
Pop	33
Souls	34
Why Keep Fighting?	34
The Fool	35
Lost Voice	36
Lost in Translation	36
What Peace do You Really Want?	37
Protecting Myself	38
Retaliation	39
Once	39
The Stuffed Cheetah	40
Love Starved	40
Permission	41
Cement Tears from a Broken Heart	41

    Floating 42

    The Humiliation 43

    What am I Actually 44

Night ii

    R. 45

    Ice Melter 45

    Exposing Myself 46

    An Enemy 47

    In No Man's Land 48

    Nonsense 49

    Rice Equals 200 50

    Why Can't They 51

    be Jealous of Me? 51

    Crying in Public 52

    Sweet 16 53

    Playing Pretend 54

    Possession at Its Finest 55

    Death and Dying 56

    What if today is the Day? 59

    Chill 60

    Red String 61

    Mother and Daughter 63

    With Lavender Tea 63

    When Death Begins with "A" 64

    Forever is too Soon 66

    Fearing *HIM* 66

    Words Won't Work 67

    Am I Your Sunshine? 67

    Alphabet 68

- My "Favorite" What If Statements 69
- The Last Time 70
- The Straight "A" Student 71
- Towards you 72
- A Planet with No Moon 73
- Spelling Bees 74
- Radio Silence 75
- Love? 76
- Leaving Again 77
- Where are You? 78
- For You Again 79
- Shattered Screens are Needed 79
- Serotonin 80
- Life 81
- Deserving 81
- You Should be Sorry 81
- Home is Gone 82
- Desperation for Him 83
- What Heartbreak does to an Author 84
- For One of My Best Friends 85
- A Staircase of Harsh Words 86
- What to do? 86
- The List is Endless 86
- S. is not always selfish 87
- Chronic 88
- A New Filter 89

Dawn iii
- War on Words 90
- Witchcraft 90

Forest Witch	90
Mary Janes and Pigtails	91
Believing	92
Ocean Eyes	93
Dear Sister,	94
Fairness	95
Piano in the Forest	95
Expect the Unexpected	95
Beauty	96
The End of an Era	96
Is Existing Enough	97
You are not just a Night Light	97
Ophelia and Orian	97
Golden Locket	98
The Days	98
Anders	99
My Little Daydreamer	100
Silver Locket	101
Whiteboards	102
Who Cares What They Think?	103
Dawn	104
Morning	**iv**
Oasis	105
Chills Across My Skin	105
Heat	105
Palm Reading	106
My Prince	106
Yet I am Loved.	107
When the Moon Finally Responds.	108

Strawberries and Sisters ... 109

Present Memories ... 110

Dear Me, before I Knew Who I Was ... 111

Precious Stones ... 112

Life Lessons from a Hardheaded Poet ... 112

If My Heart Were an Art Museum ... 113

Heaven and Hell ... 115

My Favorite Star ... 116

Meaning Everything ... 117

What Person am I in? ... 117

For My Favorite Witch ... 118

Spot the Differences ... 119

The Sun's Promise ... 120

Beautiful in His Eyes ... 121

Refusal ... 121

A Love Letter to the Little Poet I Once Was ... 122

Dusk

What's Mine

My stretch marks are *not* an invitation

to comment on my body.

My stretch marks are **mine**,

so leave them alone.

The Worth of Gold

My orgasms should be worth more than gold

To someone like you*

*words to the boys that broke me

Strung Up

I would wear it like a cut on my neck.

Like a scar down my body.

I would wear it like a noose.

Like a rope hung from my throat.

But I will not let **you** string me up.

No,

if it must happen,

it will be by my own hands.

You've lost your power.

Dear Flowers: Part Two

Dear Flowers,

That I picked when I was younger

I still don't understand why beautiful things die first.

She was beautiful.

Beauty itself personified.

But now flowers like you bud

over her precious body.

How is it fair?

The earth has her back now.

Dear Flowers,

Take care of her for us.*

*a poem for Angie.

Leaving My Home Church

Stained glass windows

        and pretty painted pictures.

You depict scenes from that book so upheld.

I'll miss you, once I'm gone.

I'll miss my church, since you left.

My Rover home forever.

I'll miss you.*

*the curse of leaving

Mushrooms

Rotting wood,

is where you grow.

But you are growing on my heart too.

Like a corpse inside,

my soul became your home.

Yet,

I love you.

Your image is etched into my mind.

You are strange.

Unique.

And beautiful.

I hope you keep growing,

But not inside.

I need you away, where I can see you sprout.

You spread slowly around me.

One day,

You will find a new home,

in the moss around the stream

right outside my mother's home.

Signed by a Lost Lover

My rose lips

—like the petals of the same name—

reach for you,

        they miss you.

What did they do,

        to form such a difference between us?

Come closer,

        hold my head in your hands.

Kiss me,

        hold my hand,

                love me with a pure fire.

Do not burn me at the stake,

        like a bonfire to warm you.

Know I love you more and more

        each time I see you.

Until I am yours,

        I am a Lost Lover

Becoming a Star

I am a candle,

        at the end of its wick.

I struggle to stay lit.

I fight to glow at night.

I shine ever so dully.

I only give off enough light

        to make out the words in my mind.

So I write them down with my melting body,

        so others can understand

               how much I once shined.

I was a candle once,

        now I am just a heavenly light

The Last Goodbye

Fake flowers, with fake dew drops.

You called what once was my church home.

I noticed you most on our last goodbye.

You looked so aged,
      so did the church.

One last goodbye.

      One last hug.

           One last blessing.

I'll miss it.

I wish you well in your unknown future*

*signed the preacher's daughter.

Colors

I cry blue tears from sea colored eyes.

I whisper pink lies from rose colored lips.

And yet you still love me.

Am I Really Enough?

You showed me her pictures.

She is so much more

than I could ever be.

So why did you pick me?

The Blessed Tomorrow

I miss the me I used to be,

        in the unhealthiest way possible.

She was sad.

        Angry.

                Lost.

Why do I miss her?

She was so bad.

I feel so much better, ~~sometimes~~

Today is a weak point.

But tomorrow will be better.

Tomorrow I see you.

Cry More

Why doesn't crying

feel as healthy

as other forms of self-care?*

*because we've been told it's not

Numbers

If age is *just a number*

then why can't weight be too?

>Pounds weigh me down more than

>the concrete blocks of your words.

Your BMI is bias,

and I call it out each time.

But,

no.

Weight can't be just a number.

But here are the numbers that **count:**

>12

>>the year that blood crawls from between

>>the legs of young girls,

>>called women before they even know why they bleed.

13%

one in eight.

An "unlucky" number.

Signifying the average hatred for one's own body.

>14

>>The age most women are lucky

>>—if they haven't been body shamed

>>for a body they never asked for.

15

this is an age when most women debate:

is this hell worth it?

to the few who say *no*…

16

you may have gotten your driver's license.

be prepared for the same joke, told time and time again:

Women can't drive.

17

this age you may have had your first partner.

your first heartbreak.

your first harassment.

18

if you make it this far, congratulations.

women are raped

far before this milestone.

19

too young to be a women

too old to be a girl

what exactly are we supposed to be?

20

lost in a space between,

we are now women

where is our respect?

21

we can drink now.

but not without our friends.

because who knows what's in our drinks.

Can weight be just a number now?

Loving Sleep

Sleep holds to you,

the way I wish to.

It surrounds you with its arms,

and you welcome it warmly.

I am not jealous of your slumber,

as I sit up in the early hours.

I listen to the sounds of the morning,

as you stay in sleep's arms.

Maybe in the Future

Hatred

is a word,

Rarely escaping from my heart.

The emotion so strongly felt

that I am blind

to what kindness the future will show.

But,

maybe in the future

I will learn to love again.

You Don't Deserve to See Me Now

If only you could see

what's become of me.

I am not the girl you left behind.

I am the Goddess of my own life.

I've Never Liked Puzzles

I want to feel whole,

in a way I don't believe I ever have.

I want to feel complete,

but completion feels so far away.

Why is it that the puzzle pieces,

are happier alone,

when they are less crowded.

Yet those same puzzle pieces,

need the others to be a complete picture.

Am I the same?

Is there such a thing?
Am I too happy?

Is that why the world shatters

so easily?

Am I too happy?

Is that why each moment with you,

no matter how long, feels like mere seconds?

Am I too happy?

Or am I pretending?

Lemon Wedges
I want to be as hard to consume as a lemon.

I am no sweet orange.

I am a bitter being.

Made by the limbs of anger.

Held by the roots of trauma.

Choke on my being.

Advice to a Younger "E"

Hello "E",

So much can be said now,

I am not you the way I was.

I am me, the way I am.

But,

If I could go back in time,

Giving you advice and warnings,

I would not.

Because the butterfly who flaps its wings

and causes a hurricane,

can be blamed the way you blame yourself.

Life will never be easy,

But you will make it through it.

Maybe not growing stronger, but I am wiser than I was.

The only advice I can give,

Being small and insignificant:

Never blame yourself fully, despite what the others say,

It is not *all* on you, but on everyone included.

Walking Horse Words

Words spoken aloud

take a new meaning

as they trot into

someone else's ears.

From Nature to Now

Like a polar bear and a penguin,

winter worlds clash with summer coats.

Wolves gather in the green

before the purple dawn of autumn.

Maroon blood stains the blue water

where the worlds meet.

War is not war in the animal kingdom,

its name is survival.

Yet,

are humans not animals

at the base of every family tree?

We keep other creatures captive,

like a ferret in a cage,

forced to listen to vinyl after vinyl

of old and new bands.

Left in silence when we humans

escape to concerts,

forgetting—just momentarily—what we left at home.

Who is more barbaric:

Man, or the polar bear?

Is our Civilization, Civilized?

Civilized?

What does that word mean?

Surely,

it cannot be used to describe

a world called today.

Surely,

it cannot be the definition

of how we humans survive.

Civilized?

Can we use that word?

Or is it like a

witch written curse?

Can we say this word?

Can we say these nine letters,

and truly, actually, mean it?

Civilized?

Are we?

What I've done to Myself

This pain,

I deserve it.

I caused it.

It's no one's fault but my own.

Yet…

How did it feel?

    Was it better for you?

        Are you happier now?

           Will I lose you because of this?

        Why didn't I speak up?

      Why am I this way?

    Why am I never good enough?

Will I ever be good enough?

Have I done enough to keep you?

Wreckage
What do I do at this point?

My world feels as though it came crashing down,

Crushing me beneath the rubble

Of my own failed dreams.

Dream Boy
Last night,

you haunted my dreams

in a way you haven't in forever:

in a nightmare.

I can't wait for you to be my daydream again.

My Sizzled Out Candle

My days are like nights now.

A constant darkness has hushed my

songbirds singing.

My starshine has gone.

My light in the darkness;

sizzled out like a candle in a hurricane.

I try to light a candle for myself,

but I burn myself with each match.

      You knew how to light the candle.

The darkness will be my comfort now;

the cold like my mistress.

Yet here I am, longing for your light.

An Ode to My Life

To the life I wish to live no longer:

I question everyday;

    "why must I suffer?"

My sins may eventually be forgiven,

    but in my life, forgiveness is scarce.

I wish to be treated equally,

    yet the golden rule is tarnished.

"Why?"

    I scream to this pitiful life.

"Why must it be this way?"

    I cry out in the silent night.

No answer ever seems to come.

    Maybe this is how it's meant to be.

Maybe this struggle will lead me forward,

    into a life full of joy and wonder.

But to leave this life behind,

    after all I've been through with it?

Leaving it abandoned,

    and forgetting what lessons I've learned?

I know how abandonment feels,

    and I will not even wish it on this life.

I know how that betrayal is,

    though I will never truly call it that.

In the end,
        this life— I wish to live no longer—is all I have.
How can I be angry at a life
        as though it has control of itself?
If I have no control of it,
        how can I expect it to?
I have no will.
        Nothing left I feel can keep me moving,
except the abandonment of my poor life,
        the betrayal of all it has.
So,
To the life I wish to live no longer,
        I will live longer with you.

The Mysterious Fossils of the Past

My childhood,

is like a mystery,

that my mind has yet to uncover.

Like a fossil,

deep within the ground,

yet to be discovered.

So don't judge me,

for a childhood,

that even *I* don't remember.

Thinning

My hair is thinning,

but I am much too young for that.

Maybe what everyone says is much too true:

I am an old soul.

An elder trapped in a young body,

as silly as that sounds.

I have no way to escape.

No exit plans.

Only a life to live,

though I feel I have lived long enough.

But I am barely an adult,

and my hair is thinning.

Life is a School

Everyone says there is a point to life,

a lesson that must be learned,

but how many lessons

until I am tired of learning new things.

Tired Again

I am tired,

in the form of an adjective,

meaning more than exhausted.

I am tired.

Tired of living,

tired of learning,

tired of existing in this single plane.

A hallelujah is not enough praise

for me to get the rest I require.

Falling to my knees will just have me slain.

And here I am,

afraid of the rest I so desperately need.

Because if I rest, so much would never get done.

I run forever,

on a worn track,

in broken soul* shoes.

I am tired.

*this is the soul I meant.

Distraction 1

Distraction works,

but only for a moment.

The cursed thoughts of you

creep back in after a few seconds.

It's not that you're not a good person,

it's just that your memory is so related to

a happiness that once was.

Sleeping Without Me

I live by counting moments,

minutes,

at night.

Darkness reigning over the light,

it is dull.

No brightness is there to comfort me,

as I cry sweet tears into my sheets.

I count the sheep,

watching them all leave

—the scene all too familiar—

then sleep retires without me.

Cocktails

I've had a cocktail in my system,

since I was 14.

I may never try a *cocktail*.

The real thing could kill me,

at least that's what the doctors have said.

So, I have to settle for the one I've got.

Because even at 21,

I'll be drink free.

Because even at 23,

My friends can go drinking

without me.

Because even at 25,

Who would remember my eyes,

as they all leave me behind?

What if I'm left behind?

Too Many Questions

What if our last conversation, was the last?

Would you regret what you said?

    Or maybe how you said it?

Would you regret your actions?

    Or at least how you hurt me?

Would you regret all the things we missed?

    Or at least have fond memories of us?

Preparation

Not even

my nightmares

prepared me

for this.

Gifts

Each gift you have given me,

    I cherish still.

Each gift you have given me,

    I hold closer to my heart.

Each gift you have given me,

    could have been the last.

Each gift I have given you,

    I will never know what will become of it.

Wishes for You

I remember,

all the wishes for love

I gave for you.

All the wishes

for your happiness.

All the wishes

for your joy.

But what have I ever gotten in return.

Abandonment

Why do I feel so abandoned?

You promised to come back.

You promised to never leave.

You promised it would be us against the world.

I trust you wouldn't lie.

But I am alone now,

wondering forever where I went wrong.

Pop

I pop my knuckles,

every few minutes

—an anxious tick—

an annoyance,

to myself and those around me.

Pop

and I do it again.

Souls

The joke has always gone:

"you've got no soul"

said each time you touch my cold hands.

I need the warmth of yours.

Because what if you were right,

and I lost my soul

years ago.

Why Keep Fighting?

I am struggling,

I am fighting for a life

that I sometimes wonder if

it is even worth living.

I know I am loved,

but it never feels

like it is enough.

Because I feel like *I* am never enough.

So why keep fighting?

Why should I keep going?

The Fool

Confusion is a fool's bliss.

The constant knowledge,

the knowing of what's happening,

the understanding of life,

it is all too much.

Yet confusion is such bliss in comparison,

because of its lack in understanding,

there is no solid knowledge

to weigh down the fool.

But to be a fool is to be a jester in the world's court,

yes, your blissful life leaves you at peace,

yet it also leaves you at the mercy,

of those who know the truth.

Confusion is a fool's bliss,

until the truth comes out.

Lost Voice
What's the point
of having a voice
when you have
no one to share
it with?

Lost in Translation
It must have been lost in translation;
on the way from my mouth to your ears,
on the way from your ears to your mind,
somewhere, something got lost.

Or maybe…

Sometime, somewhere
on the way from your mouth to my ears,
on the way from my ears to my mind,
"I hate you"
was turned around.

What Peace do You Really Want?

I was your peace.

You promised me so.

So why did you break me?

You plunged yourself into a war with life.

You let yourself fall,

and you are falling still,

what if you hurt yourself

when you finally hit the ground?

Will I still be your peace,

after all we've been through?

Let me back in,

I am begging you.

But what kind of peace do you really want?

Protecting Myself

For the people I blocked out to protect myself:

You hurt me for far too long.

You still haunt my nightmares.

You are still fresh in my mind.

But

I know you are not needed.

You were here for a lesson,

which through you, I grew.

I wish you the best in life,

though I know you curse mine

each time my name is mentioned.

I wish you well.

And please know,

I tell people the good,

at least I try my hardest to.

Because you were not all bad people.

But we were all in a bad situation.

Retaliation

Why is

it that

when I

retaliate,

I am

the worse

between us?

Once
If I didn't care,

why do you think I tried so long?

You were never a need in my life.

But you will always be missed,

because

—and I will tell everyone—

you were good, once upon a time.

The Stuffed Cheetah

I carried the stuffed cheetah with me when I left.

You gave him to me.

You helped me name him.

It is a memory I am very fond of.

But he is all I seem to have left.

Him and memories.

It will have to be enough,

because I don't know when you will come back.

A cheer to my poor plush,

for all the tears he has absorbed

and all the love he has given me.*

*poor C. Poof

Love Starved

Did I get enough love when I was young?

Is that why I am so starved for it?

Is that why each kind notion causes me to fall,

but never like how I fell for you.

I refuse to let that happen again.

Never again.

Permission

Why did you cry, my love?

Why did you cry

when you saw the outcomes

of your own actions?

Permission may be granted,

but that does not make an action wise.

Cement Tears from a Broken Heart

What I wouldn't give,

for you to feel this way too.

For you to have cement drying tears,

plastered on the side on each cheek,

gluing your eyelashes together.

But,

I still don't want this for you.

I will always want to see you happy.

I will always miss being your happiness.

Floating

My mind feels heavy,

heavier than anything

 that's ever been.

And yet,

I am still

floating away, down

and to the

unknown depths

of our lives.

The Humiliation

Love poems humiliate me.

I write them blindly,

full of joy and wonder,

full of happiness and love.

What a joke.

As though anyone would feel the same as me.

As though anyone would care.

As though the feelings are ever reciprocated.

But what if at one point,

they were?

What am I Actually

I have horns,

holding up a golden halo.

This was a joke from my family,

claiming that—though I am sweet—I am demonic.

I am a rogue spirit,

held down only by my own mind.

I run free in the fall,

held down by the hot summer.

I fly high in the spring,

held down by the freezing winter.

I am a demon,

with angel wings from my back,

and a halo held up by my horns.

so answer me this:

    what am I actually?

Night

R.

There is a word I cannot so much as whisper.

Writing its name hurts,

but it must be understood.

No one is alone in this.

I am not alone in this.

I am more than my trauma.

I am more than my pain.

Ice Melter

Break the ice

they say.

But I am a flame standing on the ice,

melting it away from under me.

Exposing Myself

Words should not be feared, yet actions can.

Rape a word that so endlessly haunts me.

"I need to move on"

    A lie. I can creep myself away from my struggles.

    Even snails get where they need to be.

"I can't keep dwelling on this forever."

    A lie and a truth. I can understand my pain, accept it even.

    But I cannot just *let go* of it in an instant.

    Even forever can seem short to a goddess.

"I'm stronger than what happened."

    A truth. I am—and will endlessly be—stronger than them.

    Yes, their actions hurt.

    But, no, they dictate me no longer.

An Enemy

"I need to eat"

No.

Food is for the beautiful.

Food is for the smart.

Food is for the fit.

Food is for everyone.

In No Man's Land

Why is my world like this:

    War.

        Hatred.

Where is it:

    Peace.

        Love.

Why are we all so:

    Mad.

        Distraught.

Where did it go:

    Happiness.

        Joy.

        And why am I in the middle still?

Nonsense

No one makes me feel as

Obsolete as the

Nightmarish person

Staring at me from my past.

Every time, every

Night. I

See you.

Everywhere.

Rice Equals 200

Rice

- *1 cup: 206 calories.*

Granola Bars

- *1 bar: 300 calories*

Gum

- *1 piece: 10 calories*

"I'm already over limit.

Rice equals 200.

The granola bar was about 300."

Don't eat the gum.

"Don't eat the gum"*

*eating disorders affect everyone.

Why Can't They be Jealous of Me?

The seed of jealousy,

grows strongly in me.

Especially when I see

she who is prettier than

I could wish to be.

I will never be sure why,

but there is no beauty in me.

At least none that I see.

Crying in Public

people stare

        they whisper.

they notice my tears.

        they hear my struggle to breathe.

they question,

        they guess:

heartbreak?

        depression?

attention seeking?

        pain?

missing someone?

but they never guess their own judgement.

Sweet 16

i watched as i slowly gave up.

i screamed from the inside

"let me be me

let me be free

let me live a life and leave me be."

but no one can hear it.

like the bit tongue i wrote of so long ago

my opinions are drowned in my blood.

the scarlet color stains the clothes I was wearing.

a t-shirt and basketball shorts.

how enticing can I be?

i was maybe sixteen…

Playing Pretend
Let's play pretend…

I am my younger self,

bright and cheerful,

young and happy.

And you,

you are the monster under my bed.

You are the big wolf

at the end of every fairytale, I've ever loved.

You didn't like playing pretend,

so you became the real villain

Possession at Its Finest

How can I find my way out?

I am constantly lost in a mind,

that I fear may not even be my own.

I am constantly hiding behind eyes,

wondering if these oceans

are even a part of my being.

Am I possessing a body

that has never been mine?

Am I the demon,

taking control?

Death and Dying

I had a class by the same name

—Psychology 4630—

my senior year of college.

I learned, from not this class alone,

how tough a passing can be,

so

I prepare this poem,

in fear of a short life,

knowing all too well,

how short life can actually be.

Trinity,

Angie,

all the little still born babies

and elders of 100.

No matter how long life is,

it is still too short to someone.

Take the dog you grew up with,

or the kitten you raised,

their lifetime to them was a lifetime long,

but to you,

it was mere years.

Take your great-grandmother and father,

their lifetime outlived wars.

But to you they didn't make it to your 20th birthday.

How could they?

Take the still born baby,

meant to greet its mother today.

Its nine months to her,

was a lifetime of nothing but love to it.

Now,

Death and Dying,

A class on how to prepare for my passing.

Not that I plan to go soon.

But like a safety net of love,

I wove this poem,

in case of the fall of my hand.

I refuse to let you tumble down,

hitting your precious head

against the cold hard ground.

But if I am not there,

promise me this one,

You will always overcome.

What if today is the Day?

Humans,

their children,

their pets,

all so fragile in a harsh lighted world.

One wrong day,

One wrong hour,

One wrong minute,

One wrong moment.

That fraction of time,

ending a lifetime of wondering

"when will death touch me?"

"when will death greet me,

take my hand and walk me home?"

What if today is the day…

Chill

"Mentally ill, but totally chill"

The words written on my favorite neon pink shirt.

A skeleton drinking coffee? Now *that's* funny!

I wear my shirt to my psychology degree.

You should see the stares,

glares all resting on me.

I smile as I pass,

Girl boss and soft whispers fill the air.

No one usually notices what I wear.

Maybe the pink is much too bright,

Or maybe the crowd knows I'm right.

But don't worry.

I'm Totally Chill.

Red String

Heaven.

It's so far away

yet so close to my fingertips.

                A pill bottle,

            split beside an empty bed.

            A cry in the silent night.

                              A car, crushed,

                            but not like my dreams

                                of our future,

                                        no,

                                more literally.

            I reach up to the clouds,

                but the you I want to hold,

                Is far beneath my feet.

Why can't I breathe?

It is like you take my breath

every time you leave.

                I am so scared of losing you,

            I forget the cicada shell of a body,

        hiding that shining soul of yours.

                                If you are gone,

                                only your body is,

                          the you that holds my heart

stays with me.

The you I love is here,

maybe not physically,

but what does that matter,

when you follow

my soul with your own.

We are tied

by that fabled red sting.

I am sure it can

stretch to heaven,

if you ever leave before me.

My love,

I will climb the red rope

up to the sky

just to touch you

one more time.

Promise me the same,

I ask,

knowing you will

climb the sky

just to get one more kiss.

Mother and Daughter

What if I were gone today.

Who would mourn my passing?

My mother?

    Of course, she would.

        She is the sun of my life

            And the sun cannot move the tides by herself.

I would regret if I left her.

    The sun tries so hard to please everyone.

        She shines so bright she may burn.

            But I, the moon, could never leave her side.

With Lavender Tea

Lavender tea.

I drink you at night,

in hopes of a restful sleep.

I lie.

I have been lying this whole time.

I speak of tea as if it is a passion of mine.

I haven't had a sip since I loved

The raspberry kind.

When Death Begins with "A"

We,

as a society,

are afraid of death.

    We are afraid of the inevitable.

We put our elderly into "homes"

    like shelter pets we grow tired of.

We shield the eyes of our children,

    hoping they will not see

        the horror that awaits them.

We send our animals "to the farm"

    yet our farmers are dying.

        Our farmlands become

            subdivision and city.

Family heirlooms have lost their names.

    My great grandmother,

        a name I can barely remember,

        but I am like her.

I am a repeated pattern

    in the quilted home of my last name.

But when my last name is no long my own,

    will my past still stay with me?

Or when I grow old,

    will my present disappear?

My family has that history.

    The loss of mind.

        Or the loss of function.

ALS and Alzheimer's,

    the only "A" names

        I fear.

I am scared.

    What if I forget my life,

        my love,

            my family?

What if I remember the world,

    But the world forgets me?

What if I am never remembered,

when my death begins with "A"

Forever is too Soon

"It's been a while,

you've been gone for months now.

So,

why did you come back?"

Who said we would ever stay away?

Who said we were finished with what we started?

Seeing you this way is our purpose,

so,

where were we?

Where did we leave off?

Do you want to play a game?

Fearing *HIM*

Is it your hands

I feel around my neck?

Is it your breath I feel

down me?

Is it your heat

against my back?

I hope not…

Words Won't Work

I made you cry,

two days in a row.

I never meant to hurt you.

The pain I caused was uncalled for;

jealousy is just an evil demon.

I'm sorry,

though words will never fix what I've caused.

I'm sorry.

Am I Your Sunshine?

You cried on my shoulder.

I cried against your head.

I could smell your shampoo, your cologne.

Your soft sigh as you let the hurt out

hurt me more than I will ever admit.

Your tears were so cold,

my heart froze over with one drop.

The artic has more life

than my soul did in that moment.

Let me be your Sunshine again.

Alphabet

Hypotheticals are like, when as a child,

we learned about the alphabet.

One letter blends into another,

making each word.

One-word trails into another,

making ropes to tangle around my pale throat.

One rope ties to another,

making a noose, perfect fit for me.

The letters blur together,

the words bleed away.

Why can't I be happy?

Why am I this way?

My "Favorite" What If Statements
"Hypothetically Speaking"

The words start my favorite *what if* statements.

What if I were finally enough for someone?
> Well, I was, for a while.
> It was heaven for months.
> It was hell for weeks.

What if I were finally happy?
> Well, I was, for a while.
> Then, I made a mistake.
> And ruined it for everyone.

What if I were finally healthy?
> Well, I was, for a while.
> But then something happened,
> Though I'm not sure what.

What if I weren't a mistake?
> What if I never made any?
> What if I were perfect?
> What if I were something good.

Well, *Hypothetically Speaking*…

The Last Time

I dare you to say it again.

I dare you to mean it again.

I have such a growing fear,

that you may never truly mean it again.

What if I'm right?

What if the last time,

was the last time,

you truly meant

I love you.

The Straight "A" Student

An "A" is worth more,

than my own being.

      Anxiety creeps in.

My grades are slipping,

my mind slips faster.

      Depression takes a slow waltz into my life.

What is my worth?

Now that I am no longer gifted,

    I see none.

I struggle now.

I am no perfect student,

    nor a perfect person.

I struggle with my self-worth.

    I struggle with who I am meant to be.

Because if I am not a perfect student,

    how can I be?

Towards you

I want to be bitter.

I want to be angry.

I want to be hateful.

But I can't,

not towards you.

Not towards you, my love.

        Just not towards you.

A Planet with No Moon

I am alone now.

    This world has no one for me.

I know there are people who care

    but where are they when I need them?

I need to respect their time,

    their lives;

        no one's world revolves around me.

I am a planet with no moon

    nothing to help change my tides,

        my gravitational pull

            holds nothing to me.

Even my tears float away.

Yes,

    I have a sun,

        She is bright and beautiful,

            but she is not always what I need.

I need to become my own moon;

    but how can I live two lives in one?

I see a meteor coming for me.

I see it breaking me,

but I still see my survival.

Spelling Bees

Dry spells,

when spelling is hard.

When my writing

becomes so difficult to express,

that it stays better in my mind alone.

But my mind is a dangerous place for words.

My mind is a dangerous place.

The little spelling bees,

they come to the hive of my mind,

but my hive is a wasp's nest.

A trap for my poor, beloved creatures.

I set them free on the page,

As quickly as I can.

Stay safe, little ones.

Radio Silence

Radio silence.

My least favorite thing.

Only because I know,

you could reach out,

yet you choose not to.

This isn't the first time you've done this.

At least last time you cut me out officially.

Yet here I am,

once again,

waiting for you to come back.

Please come back…

Love?

I hate how I love you

with the same passion of the past.

Yet where are you now;

now that I need someone in my life.

Now that I have no one.

Silence is all I have left.

And silence has never loved me.

Only you have.

Leaving Again

I always will wonder

        what is wrong with me.

I wait for you time and time again.

        Yet you leave.

You leave me.

        After every promise you've made.

Yes, I am flawed.

        I have broken promises too.

But never one that strong.

        Never one like that.

You say you'll never leave.

        But where are you now?

Gone.

I'm not sure for how long,

        but every second is a lifetime longer.

What is so wrong with me,

        to prompt you to this response.

I don't know why I still wait.

        I will be here,

when you get back.

        But will I be the same?

Where are You?

Why am I so angry with you?

    Yes, you've hurt me,

        but I've hurt you.

Maybe not as bad,

    but no one

        should compare traumas.

You've missed so much in just two days.

    From all my childish joy.

        To all the screaming and crying.

You've missed so much in just two days.

    I've tried to ignore this feeling,

        but this feeling is abandonment.

Through all your troubles

    I have been there for you.

        I have supported you.

Where is my support?

    Where is my loyalty?

        Where is my love?

Where are you?

For You Again

I wish,

once again,

for a life full of love for you.

Knowing I once was,

but may never be again.

Shattered Screens are Needed

I wish the screen of my phone

was shattered.

That way each notification I check,

looking for your name,

will hurt just as bad as it does inside.

Blood never really scared me.

But losing you always has.

And I don't know where you are now.

Serotonin

Serotonin.

The "happy chemical".

The partial cause of most mental illnesses.

How can you be so good,

yet be so bad?

You're like my love.

Too much is bad,

not enough is bad.

But if you find a happy medium,

I make you happier than anyone ever could.

Life

life

is

not

what

it

should

be.

Deserving
I've been true to you.

Acting as though I deserve the same.

But life, again, has proven to me,

no matter what I feel I deserve:

I will never deserve it.

You Should be Sorry
I wish you would take responsibility.

Not for what you've done,

you've already admitted that.

No,

but for how you made me feel.

You seem to know how much you've hurt me,

but it still happens.

Are you even sorry?

Home is Gone

The feelings come in waves,

like an ocean in a hurricane.

Abandoned　　　　　　*Abandoned*

　　　Alone　　　*Alone*　　　*Alone*

　　　　　　Forgotten　　　　　　*Forgotten*

I feel homeless,

while under the blanket in my bed.

Not because there is no roof over my cold head.

Rather,

home is where your heart is,

and you walked away with mine.

Desperation for Him

I reek of death.

    Though my death is years ahead,

        Death hears me each time I call his name.

    I call for him in desperation.

And here I sit, alone.

What Heartbreak does to an Author

Slowly,

you are losing me.

Once,

I would have traded all the writing in the world,

to see you for an hour.

Now,

I write about you,

just like I used to.

What happened?

Why is it like this?

Why must I hurt?

What pain am I feeling?

I don't know how to feel.

For One of My Best Friends

You were a good friend,

for a long time.

        I will never say you weren't.

But people change,

you did.

As did I.

I don't blame you,

but I know some blame can lean on you.

It is not *all* your fault.

But you disregarded me.

Lied to someone,

Though I'm not sure who.

Left me for my love.

You abandoned me.

So,

I will leave your life,

happily,

to make you feel as though you've won.

But please understand,

you will be missed,

but it is all your loss.

A Staircase of Harsh Words
Take

    accountability

        for

            all

                the

                    wrong

                        you've

                            done

                                to me.

What to do?
What if you never come back?

What if all those promises,

were nothing but a ploy to silence me?

What if you *do* come back,

but nothing is ever the same again?

What will I do then?

The List is Endless
I will

take accountability,

for all

the things

wrong with me.

S. is not always selfish

It isn't an escape.

    It isn't an "easy way out".

        It isn't a five second fix to a lifetime of problems.

    It isn't a way to leave everyone behind.

It isn't a way to hurt others.

You see,

when I say **suicide**

—that cursed word makes people jump back—

I do not mean any of those things above.

I mean the monster that rots good peoples' minds.

I mean the monster that makes people think:

    Everyone would be better without me.

    Everyone's life would be better if I never existed.

How can I get it through some hardheaded skulls:

Suicide is not *always* selfish.

It is what the lost soul thinks that causes it.

The "better without me"

is the killer.

Chronic

An adjective with so much meaning.

Recurring, long-lasting, and persisting,

something that seems impossible to get rid of.

A physical illness can be chronic,

seen or unseen by the public.

Judged or unjudged by that same public.

A mental illness can be chronic,

always unseen by most,

seen only by those who stand close.

Why won't people see mental health too?

A New Filter
You've been making things harder.

    I know you never mean to.

        But learn to filter what you say.

Dawn

War on Words

"I am beautiful"

my mind wages war

on those words.

But

I know my truth.

Witchcraft

If my mother were a witch,

I would burn down the town

before the flames could ever touch her.

Forest Witch

Why can I only dance around my pains,

like I am the forest witch

who dances around her fire.

Am I afraid to get burned,

or am I afraid of the truth?

Mary Janes and Pigtails

I like wearing:

- Mary Janes
    - **With** ruffle socks
- A cute black dress
    - Possibly the one with mushrooms
- Pigtails
    - Sometimes with little bows or barrettes

This is my inner child,

      Finally finding the room to be her dream self.

This is me,

      Reliving a childhood I don't remember.

So why stare?

Why judge me for a past you don't even know?

Let me be my inner child.

    Let me be My Inner Child.

        Let me be ME.*

*signed by the child deep inside my mind.

Believing

"Beauty is in my own life, especially in the mirror."

    Repeat it.

        Repeat it.

            Repeat it.

"Beauty is in my own eyes."

    Repeat it.

        Repeat it.

            Repeat it.

"Beauty is my second name."

    Repeat it.

        Repeat it.

            Repeat it.

Now,

    Believe it.

Ocean Eyes

Ocean eyes,

        ocean eyes.

Never cry,

        my pretty ocean eyes.

Never drown.

        in your own sad sorrow.

Shining ocean eyes,

        let me find the treasure inside.

Dear Sister,

I have never written a poem about you.

You and I have a history.

Like in the stories of great wars,

      we fought,

           we battled,

but in the end you are my only sister.

You are the only one I want.

No one can ever replace you.

Through everything, it's us against the world.

Fight for me,

      not with me.

           and I will fight for you.

Let's fight the world together.*

*signed a younger sister, who lover her older sister.

Fairness
Men don't cry.

Only because we don't let them.

    Only because we call them weak.

        Only because we laugh at them.

But men have emotions too.

It's about time we let them feel it.*

*it's only fair.

Piano in the Forest

My walk through the forest,

Cut short by the mysterious music.

I follow the sound,

A trance encapsulating me.

There she is,

Like a piano in the forest,

She stands out against the green of the world.

Expect the Unexpected

I never know what to expect in life,

But the unexpected is a hidden blessing.

I didn't expect to meet you.

Beauty

I am beautiful. I am beautiful. I am beautiful. I am beautiful. I am beautiful. I am beautiful. I am beautiful. I am beautiful. I am beautiful. I am beautiful. I am beautiful. I am beautiful. I am beautiful. I am beautiful. I am beautiful. I am beautiful. I am beautiful.*

*I'm glad you finally admitted it

The End of an Era

Cassettes' dreams

and records' screams

signify the end of their era.

Their death like my own,

as I beg for them to hold to life.

No song sounds better

than with the soft crackle

of scars

on each of my records.

No sound is as sweet

as the rewind of my favorite tape.

My phone holds more songs than I own records,

but I will miss them,

after their era.

Is Existing Enough
How I

    wish we

        could just

            exists in

                this world.

You are not just a Night Light
                You promised me,

            not long ago,

        if one of us were to go,

      we would haunt the other's life,

                  darling,

          you are my favorite light.

Ophelia and Orian
My aid,

my benefit.

My sunrise,

my golden dawn.

Predict my future

as I read the old old cards.

Answer my inquires,

and help me tread on.

Golden Locket

I lost something dear to me,

more than one thing I suppose.

The first to mind

is my mother's golden locket.

It had a picture of when my family

was a "family",

a show for other people.

A mask of what we truly were.

Now my family is a *family*,

No matter how broken we are.

I just wish I knew where my locket was.

To show just how far,

we've actually come.

The Days

Dawns always are too bright.

Mornings always come too soon.

Dusks always hide my light.

Nights always last too long.

Yet here I am,

In this cycle.

Anders

Strength is something I have always lacked.

It is like Strength, as a being, is hiding from me.

For the purpose of my health,

we will name him Anders.

He looks away from me often,

even when I scream his name.

Every crack in my voice makes him flinch,

my cries are gunshots to him,

though I am the one with bullet holes.

Anders claims to love everyone,

even those weaker.

Yet my weakness sickens him.

He gags on the scent of my sadness.

So,

Anders,

why must you hide from me.

Reveal yourself so that I may be like you.

Show me who I should be.

My Little Daydreamer

Daydreamer,

my little lover,

stay strong just a little longer.

Daydreamer,

I see you crying,

cry into my loving shoulder.

Daydreamer,

cry no longer,

the sun is still shining.

Daydreamer,

go play outside,

the clouds are away from the sky.

Daydreamer,

my little lover,

stay in love with me.

Silver Locket

My mother's locket is still missing,

but I gained something I love.

A gift from my love,

a little silver locket,

with two pictures inside.

On the outside,

the little pink flower

—beside a mirror like surface—

is rough then smooth

between my two fingers.

This locket is my own,

a show that I am grown,

yet my childlike wonder is never gone.

I love the shiny exterior,

and I love the light-colored photos.

But I do not love it as much as you.

Whiteboards

A whiteboard of love,

is in my mother's office.

It makes me wonder what words would be said,

if my heart were a whiteboard.

Would the markers stain my heart,

with negative words.

Would my sleeves erase the kindest of them,

when I dry my worst tears.

My whiteboard heart

would have colorful letters,

each a note of compassion.

I know I am loved in my life,

but sometimes I feel blind.

Write kind words on my whiteboard heart,

because I need a reminder,

that I am not blind.

Who Cares What They Think?

What if people stop seeing me

for who I think I am?

But what does that even matter?

I know *who* I am,

they do not.

I know *how* I am,

they do not.

And if they fail to see me,

and how I have treated them with the kindness I have;

if they only see the wrong I have done,

that is their fault,

not mine.

Dawn

The sunlight starts trickling

through my window again.

I love when I am awake for the colors.

When I worked the night shift at my first job,

My favorite part of the days was each time

The sun peaked through the horizon.

The sun left streaks of pastels across the sky,

She welcomed me outside, each time.

Even on those cold, icy days.

Morning

Oasis

Every crack and crevice

where my sweat sets,

is like a waterfall centered garden

where flowers are yet to be.

Chills Across My Skin

Cold air kisses my skin,

much like you do.

Both leave chills across my body.

Heat

The heat of you,

pressed against me.

Your breath,

warm against my neck.

Soft snores lure me to sleep.

Your love surrounds me endlessly.

Palm Reading

I found my happiness somewhere

I never thought I would,

never thought I could.

But even the witches can't read the future

when my palm is pressed against yours.

My Prince

I feel secure with you.

Like you are the castle walls to protect me

from my own mind.

Like you are my prince in shining armor

to rescue me from the tower of sadness.

Yet I am Loved.
I am not perfect.

Yet,

I am Loved.

I am not happy, like I should be.

Yet,

I am Loved.

I am not honest with myself.

Yet,

I am Loved.

If not by you, then by me.

When the Moon Finally Responds.

I asked the moon,

"how come you don't heat the world?

Is it because you are less glorious than the sun?"

Her answer: was sad, yet sweet

If everyone heated the world,

Would there be a world left?

We each do what we need.

I light the night for the animals and sleepless humans.

I pull the sea's tides, moving the water for the world.

I am no more or less glorious than she who outshines me.

I am important just the same.

As are you.

Strawberries and Sisters

I do not like your taste.

It is either too sweet or too tart.

I like your color,

    it is beautiful

        like your buds—before you bloom.

Your aesthetic,

    I flaunt it often.

        I love the way you look.

Your shine is addictive.

    As are you.

Continue to grow in my heart.

    Let me take you home to share with my sister.

She will love you more,

    than I ever will.

But I will love her more than you can.

    She outshines you in my mind.

I will forever put her first.

I will give her all of my strawberries.*

*when you miss your sister.

Present Memories

Memories are a gift,

        given by angels.

a gift given by the one's you love.

        a present from the past.

a present from the moment.

You are my favorite memory.

        Be my moment forever.

Dear Me, before I Knew Who I Was

I know you, my dear.

You had so many escape plans.

So many 'what if's floating in your mind.

But,

'what if' I told you happiness exists?

What if I told you the life of your dreams

is just around a hidden corner.

The bad comes before the good.

The forest fire leads to new growth.

Your body changes, but you still don't love it.

But you,

now,

the one I am writing this for,

never knew how much it meant to say

"I am Beautiful"

and actually mean it.

I was lost when I was you,

but I found myself,

through what was left of you.

Thank You*

*Signed the newly found

Precious Stones

Emeralds and opals will

never mean more to me than you.

Life Lessons from a Hardheaded Poet

- Use your heart—not your head—when writing
    - Poetry is about the emotions you feel and create, not about the words you write.
- Enjoy the world, don't just live in it.
    - From lavender macarons to bird songs, life is worth living.
- If you keep your eyes forward, your heart will wander.
    - Focusing on one thing may drive your heart to find something new.
- If you are just okay, that's okay.
    - Okay is a pretty good thing compared to bad.
- Stand your ground, but don't sink into it.
    - Make sure your ground is solid, don't find yourself on the wet sand.

More lessons to come,

    when they are learned.

If My Heart Were an Art Museum

If my heart,

were an art museum,

I would affectionately call it

"A Life Unknown".

Not because I do not know my own life,

no,

because those on the outside do not.

Each section,

a part of my life I wish I could forget,

a part of my life I wish to cling to forever.

From what happened with ~~him~~

to what is happening with **him.**

~~He~~ is a demon.

A beast which belongs in shackles.

I would keep ~~him~~ on display.

Because that monster deserves nothing,

but a life of my revenge.

He is an angel.

A heavenly being

that carries me through the air.

He treats me like the goddess I believe I am.

He acknowledges my growth.

I would not keep **him** in my museum.

I would keep **him** by my side,

forever to hold my hand,

to keep me steady as we walk.

In "A Life Unknown"

statues and paintings would line the halls,

moments of time,

frozen in the minute.

From the moment of my birth,

To the second of my death.

I am glad my heart

is not an art museum.

Because my heart is *mine* and mine alone.

Heaven and Hell

When the sky falls down,

and the Garden of Eden

touches her feet on the earth

once more,

when the earth cracks open,

and hell opens her hand

to touch the fresh grass

with morning dew

then,

and only then,

will I stop loving you.

Who is the Hero?

The hero to the ant,

is the villain

to the anteater.

My Favorite Star

You still are my sunshine.

The clouds may have blocked
your shining smile from my eyes.

The clouds may have rained your tears
down on the dry trampled dirt.

But I know flowers can grow
from the darkness of your mind.

You will always be my favorite star.

Meaning Everything

Careful with your words, my darling.

Careful with your eyes, my love.

They say things you try to hide.

Your sadness for one.

    I wish I could hush that mind of yours.

    It screams as loud as mine, sometimes.

You deserve better.

You deserve happiness, in a way I may never be able to give.

    You, my dearest, mean everything.

What Person am I in?

The few memories I have,

seem to be in third person.

Yet all my writing, is in first.

Is this my minds way,

of making up for its flaws;

or its way of protecting me

from unknown traumas?

What things am I forgetting?

What memories have I lost?

And

why does it feel

like I can't forgive my mind?

For My Favorite Witch

To the people,

who call my mother a witch:

You only say so,

in fear of what she is capable of.

You only say so,

because the new is frightening.

You only say so,

because the other word seems too harsh

for your work setting.

Woman up,

or chicken out.

Because this witch is on her side.

Spot the Differences

My life is like a crystal quartz,

        playing itself off as a diamond.

No,

        the other way around.

My life is like a diamond,

        playing itself off as a crystal quartz.

While both are beautiful,

        one is made to seem more important.

Its rarity is like my own.

        My life may have similarities,

but my life is never to be copied.

The Sun's Promise

My mother,

the sun I write of so often,

cried with me.

She listened to how I spoke

of an abandoned soul,

a heart broken into millions.

But she made a promise,

tears in her eyes:

I will stay until you say you don't need me,

I'll only go if you are ready.

If only my sun could shine forever.

Beautiful in His Eyes
If God

truly does

see beauty

in everything,

does that

make me

beautiful too?

Refusal
I refuse.

I refuse to let this break me.

I refuse to let this hurt me any longer.

I refuse to take this awful planet,

with all these awful people,

and offer love to everyone.

Not everyone deserves a piece of me.

But I deserve me as a whole.

I refuse to believe otherwise.

A Love Letter to the Little Poet I Once Was

A love letter, to the little poet I once was.

We grew out our hair,

something we were very insecure about.

Then we outgrew it.

Our hair is still long,

but it no longer reaches past our waist.

We miss it,

but we feel so much freedom now.

But no freedom like in our little world.

No one found our secret,

I know you were scared they would.

People say our little portals were birthed from nothing more

than an *overactive imagination*.

But we know the truth,

our world is still out there,

we just lost the keys.

I want to go back to those colors.

The "real" world is much too dull.

It is like a black and white cartoon,

but no one is happy

and there are no choreographed songs.

Just too much silence.

And the dark takes over.

The more we begin to write,

the realer everything becomes.

Our "imagination"

is no longer under *our* control.

It seems as though we had it on a chain

for too long.

Poking and prodding it with our ideas.

But then it caged us,

throwing the carcass of our childhood memories

through the bars and into our face.

What was it like to be you?

I have forgotten what your smile was like,

Was it sweet?

Like the candied kisses from him I dream of?

Or sweet like the roses from our first bouquet?

What was it like to be you?

I have a childhood

that I cannot seem to remember.

It fails me,

each time my memory tries.

It fails to tell me the joys I *must* have experienced.

We were happy then.

Tell me we were happy.

I act as though I expect a response from some one

who I do not even remember.

I find evidence of your existence though.

Through yearbooks and old writings.

You loved poetry just like me,

it is a part of our blood.

So,

why can't I see you.

I try so hard looking back,

all I see is darkness.

Splashes of half memories come and go,

But where are you,

little poet?

Where did I lose you?

Other books by E.E. Sorrells:

- With Raspberry Tea (published 2021)
- With Sassafras Tea (published 2023)

If you made it this far...

Readers like you have lit up my world! I appreciate every way you've supported me, and I hope you will continue to far into the future. Thank you for letting me write my heart out and thank you for reading my work. Please support me on social media @e.e.sorrells

The support from you all have made a world of difference for me. I cannot wait to see who all finds my book. Happy reading in the future!

-E.E. Sorrells

www.ingramcontent.com/pod-product-compliance
Lightning Source LLC
Chambersburg PA
CBHW042127100526
44587CB00026B/4198